CREATIVE LIVES

Pablo Picasso

JEREMY WALLIS

Heinemann
LIBRARY

www.heinemann.co.uk/library
Visit our website to find out more information about **Heinemann Library** books.

To order:
☎ Phone 44 (0) 1865 888066
▤ Send a fax to 44 (0) 1865 314091
▭ Visit the Heinemann Bookshop at www.heinemann.co.uk/library to browse our
catalogue and order online.

First published in Great Britain by Heinemann Library, Halley Court, Jordan Hill, Oxford
OX2 8EJ, a division of Reed Educational and Professional Publishing Ltd. Heinemann is a
registered trademark of Reed Educational & Professional Publishing Ltd.

OXFORD MELBOURNE AUCKLAND JOHANNESBURG BLANTYRE
GABORONE IBADAN PORTSMOUTH NH (USA) CHICAGO

Designed by Tinstar Design (www.tinstar.co.uk)
Originated by Ambassador Litho Ltd.
Printed and bound in Hong Kong/China

ISBN 0 431 13983 0
05 04 03 02 01
10 9 8 7 6 5 4 3 2 1

British Library Cataloguing in Publication Data
Wallis, Jeremy
      Pablo Picasso. – (Creative lives)
      1.Picasso, Pablo, 1881-1973 – Juvenile literature
      2.Painters – Spain – Biography – Juvenile literature
      I.Title
      759.6

Acknowledgements
The Publishers would like to thank the following for permission to reproduce photographs:
AKG: pp7, 10, 25, 43, 51, 55; Archives de la Fondation Erik Satie: p28; Art Institute of Chicago: p35;
Bridgeman Art Library: pp5, 18, 20, 40, 48, 52; Courtesy of the Trustees of the V&A: p49; Guggenheim
Museum, New York: p15; Metropolitan Museum of Art: pp20, 22; Musée Picasso, Paris: pp13, 19, 23, 26,
29, 36, Michele Bellot p39, J.G. Berizzi pp33, 34, Coursaget p31, J Faujour p17, Beatrice Hatala p44, Herve
Lewandowski p53; Museu Picasso, Barcelona: p12; Museum of Modern Art, New York: pp42, 47.

Cover photograph reproduced with permission of Hulton Getty.

Our thanks to Richard Stemp for his comments in the preparation of this book.

Every effort has been made to contact copyright holders of any material reproduced in
this book. Any omissions will be rectified in subsequent printings if notice is given to
the Publisher.

Disclaimer
All the Internet addresses (URLs) given in this book were valid at the time of going to press. However,
due to the dynamic nature of the Internet, some addresses may have changed, or sites may have ceased
to exist since publication. While the author and Publisher regret any inconvenience this may cause
readers, no responsibility for any such changes can be accepted by either the author or the Publisher.

Any words appearing in the text in bold, **like this**, are explained in the Glossary.

Contents

Who was Pablo Picasso?

Pablo Picasso was the most famous artist of the 20th century and one of the greatest of all time. A technically brilliant artist, he remade himself many times as an artistic visionary, until the very end of his life, aged 92 years. The extraordinary events of his life gradually took on a near legendary quality, until Picasso resembled a character from one of the Greek myths he loved so much.

Picasso lived his life publicly. He was the first 'world artist' in the age of celebrity, when the media – newspapers, magazines, newsreels, film, television and radio – communicated his works, words and deeds around the world. He took inspiration from wherever he found it: from his Catholic upbringing, African artefacts, the art of the Pacific Islands, the **primitive** works of his Spanish forebears, the pervasive Islamic influence in Spain, and from his lovers and the events that convulsed the world during his lifetime.

By avoiding association with any single 'movement' or 'school' of art Picasso avoided labels. He leapt like a grasshopper from phase to phase. He was endlessly inventive, endlessly controversial, and attracted fanatical devotion and derision in equal measure. People who know his work love it or loathe it – with Picasso, there is no 'middle way'.

Understanding Picasso

It is important to study Picasso the man – understanding his life and character is vital in grasping his art. The reverse is also true – to know the man, it is important to know and understand his art. Each of Picasso's advances in technique, interpretation and style were accompanied by a fracture or dislocation in his personal life. His happiness (or otherwise) in his relationships with others profoundly influenced his work. Every time Picasso broke with his own artistic precedents, he also broke with huge parts of his past life – wives, lovers, children, homes and friends.

In many ways Pablo Picasso remains a mystery. He developed a reputation both as a great artist and as a man who could be very cruel to his lovers and wives. To find Picasso the man, behind the myth of Picasso the creator and Picasso the monster, we also must pick our way through a maze of his own design.

Self-Portrait with Coat, 1901. Pablo Picasso aged 20, an artist on the verge of greatness at the dawn of the 20th century.

Picasso's early life

On 25 October 1881, Pablo Ruiz y Picasso was born dead. Set aside by the midwife, he was saved by his uncle's quick thinking: leaning over, Don Salvador blew a lungful of cigar smoke into the infant's face. The great artist Picasso entered life with a grimace and a shriek of fury. He would later claim his birth was the source of his **hypochondria** and fear of illness.

Pablo's father, Don José Ruiz, was a charming dreamer and an artist. He worked as **curator** of the Municipal Museum in Málaga, in the Spanish province of Andalucia. In Doña Maria Picasso López, seventeen years his junior, he found a wife with the steely determination he lacked. They married in December 1880. Within a month, Maria was pregnant with Pablo.

Little Pablo – or Pablito as everyone called him – lived in a crowded house with his parents, Maria's unmarried sisters and widowed mother. Though not wealthy, it was a respectable, middle-class and cultured household. Everyone fussed over the handsome Pablito. 'He was an angel and a devil in beauty,' his mother said.

From Don José, Pablo learned the basics of art. José particularly liked to paint doves and Picasso would claim he always associated them with a child-like sense of peace, innocence and hope. 'There were always doves around… captured in the dining-room pictures.' Before he could speak, Picasso made his wishes known by drawing, discovering he could earn sugared fritters – *churros* – simply by drawing them. His first word was *'Piz!'* – short for *lapis*, meaning pencil. Picasso also shared his father's passion for the bullfight.

> **"** Picasso's mother, Doña Maria Picasso López, once said to him: *'If you become a soldier, you will be a general. And if you become a monk, you will be the pope.* **"**

Life in Málaga

Picasso spent his early years in Málaga, where a steep rocky mount with an *alcázar* (castle) at the top dominates the town. In December 1884, Málaga was shaken by an earth tremor. José led his pregnant wife and Pablo to a friend's house built into the rock below the castle. There, Maria gave birth to Pablo's sister, Dolorès (or Lola, as she would always be known). His sister's sudden arrival, in the midst of this storm of dirt and fear, had a profound impact on the little boy: he was no longer the sole object of everyone's attention!

From the castle rock, you can still see the bullring, the cathedral and the churches in the town. Picasso remembered many scenes from this time in his life: the melancholic Spanish Catholicism, the tortured figure of Christ crucified that adorned the churches, the spectacle of *Semana Santa* (Easter Holy Week), and the pageantry of the bullfights he enjoyed – all are powerful images that appear over and over again in his work.

Early signs of talent

As a child, Pablo cut out the shapes of animals, people and flowers and projected them on to a wall.

Pablo Picasso at fifteen. Though already a skilled artist, Pablo's difficulty with words and numbers made him a very unhappy pupil at school.

7

In his cousins, he found a keen audience: 'draw us a dog, a chicken…
a donkey!' In 1888, Picasso began to paint under his father's tuition.
At the same time his progress in other subjects at school was very
poor. By the age of six he so hated school that a maid had to drag
him bodily through the streets and right into the classroom.

In 1891, Don José accepted a teaching post at the School of Fine Arts
in Coruña, in Galicia province. Pablo seemed to settle well there. With
his new friends, he organized mock bullfights and hunted the street
cats. While Pablo continued to show remarkable talent as an artist,
he could not make sense of numbers or words. Instead of numbers
he saw shapes: 7 was an upside-down nose, 2 was a woman kneeling
in prayer, 4 was a sailboat on the ocean. He could not see them as
numbers with a value. It is now thought he had a form of **dyslexia**.

In 1892, Pablo was accepted as a student at the School of Fine Arts,
where his father taught. He was only ten years old. His talent was
prodigious, his subjects adult: nudes, figures from mythology, portraits
and landscapes. 'I had never done children's drawings,' Picasso later
declared. Of an exhibition of children's art, he said, 'I could not have
taken part. When I was twelve, I was drawing like Raphael.' (For more
on Raphael, see page 59.)

Defining moments

In 1895, when Pablo was thirteen, his eight-year-old sister,
Concepción, who everyone called Conchita, contracted **diphtheria**.
Picasso made a desperate pact with God: he would not paint again if
God saved Conchita. On 10 January she died. Pablo decided God
was evil, but at the same time felt terribly guilty. He was torn between
wanting his sister saved, but not wanting to surrender his art. Though
guilt-stricken, Pablo became convinced that Conchita's death
represented God's permission for him to dedicate his life to art.

Not long after Conchita's death, Pablo's father asked Pablo to paint
some pigeons' feet as part of a picture while he went out. When he
returned, Pablo had finished. Don José immediately handed his

palette, paints and brushes to the boy. He would paint no more, he announced, the son had overtaken the father.

That same year Don José secured a teaching post at the Barcelona School of Fine Arts. He wanted Pablo admitted as a senior student. Candidates had a month to complete the entrance exam. Famously, Picasso claimed he completed it in a day. (The works he submitted actually have two separate dates, but it was a remarkable achievement for a fourteen-year-old. The examiners awarded him their highest marks.)

Though Picasso claimed the teachers could not teach him anything and that he owed nothing to the **Great Masters**, the technical training he received gave him a solid foundation for his artistic development. Picasso's rebelliousness was in keeping with the times: the fast-approaching 20th century stimulated rebellion everywhere.

Spain in turmoil

Throughout Spain in the 1890s, while Pablo was growing up, people demanded change. They believed the **monarchy** and church had failed them and had cheated them. In the countryside, peasants who worked all day for a loaf of bread rose in revolt. In the towns, intellectuals rejected the old political, cultural and artistic conventions and working people demanded rights and freedoms. **Socialism**, powerful outside Spain, grew in influence, while **anarchism** was more powerful here than anywhere else. In provinces such as Catalonia and the Basque region, many saw themselves as separate peoples and yearned for independence.

Throughout Spain, people looked at the economic, social and political progress made in France, Britain, Germany and the USA, and were desperate to drag Spain into the 20th century. Many artists sympathized with this.

Growing up and moving on

Picasso persuaded his father to set him up in his own studio, where he painted *Science and Charity*. The writer Denis Thomas called it the 'last work of his boyhood, and… the first… of his manhood'. Picasso composed many pictures on religious themes. While he rejected organized religion, Picasso often used Christ's tortured figure as a symbol of suffering.

Many of his paintings at this time were reproductions of other artists' work – especially of the French artist Toulouse-Lautrec (see page 59) and the English Pre-Raphaelite Brotherhood. However, he knew little of the **Impressionists**.

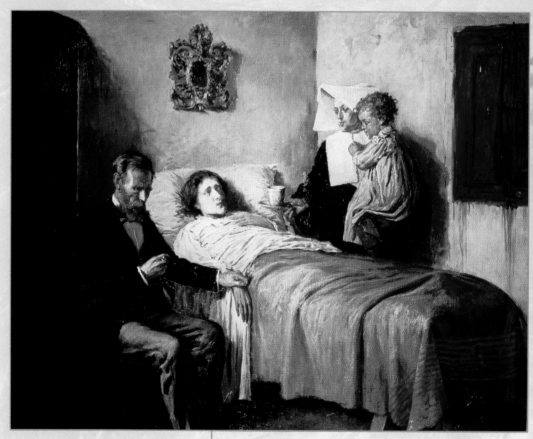

Science and Charity, 1897. Pablo's father modelled as the doctor. The painting won an Honourable Mention at an art exhibition in Madrid, before being given to Pablo's uncle, Don Salvador.

The Pre-Raphaelite Brotherhood

The Pre-Raphaelite Brotherhood were a group of artists who formed in London in 1848. Their intention was to revolutionize Victorian art and reinvent painting in the style of 15th century artists – that is Italian painters *before* Raphael. They wanted to paint serious subjects and to study nature closely. Members of the PRB, as they became known, avoided heavy shadows in their work and rejected the dark and murky style of other artists working at the time. Instead they painted with bright colours on a white background. They became known for their hard-edged forms, their realism and attention to detail.

At this time, Pablo's attitude to his father changed. Don José nurtured his son's talent, but Pablo resented his father's constructive criticism and advice. He preferred his mother's unthinking and absolute adoration of his charm and abilities. It was Picasso, her family name, which he adopted. When Pablo enrolled at the Royal Academy in Madrid in 1897, still aged only sixteen, he denied his father's role as his teacher. He completed his entrance tests in a day. His extended family pooled their resources to fund his studies.

While in Madrid, Picasso visited the national collection of art at the Prado Museum. This opened his eyes to the work of Velázquez, Van Dyck and El Greco (see pages 58–59). However, the Academy disappointed him: he found the style of instruction boring. Instead, he preferred to roam the streets and squares or spend his time in bars and **bordellos** watching people. A tutor at the Royal Academy, who was also a friend of his father, reported Pablo's absenteeism, his lack of work and his poor attitude. His relatives cut his allowance off. Only his father continued to send money. Too poor even to rent a studio, Pablo was reduced to painting in the open air. In spring 1898, illness provided the excuse he needed to leave.

Illness and recovery

A painter friend, Manuel Pallarés, invited Pablo to recuperate in his village, Horta de Ebro, in the Catalan mountains. Picasso would stay there for six months. Creating stories about his past, Picasso later described it as a lost paradise: 'All I know I learned in the village where Pallarés was born.'

Manuel and Pablo travelled into the mountains, with a young gypsy guide, to paint. Picasso later claimed that the gypsy taught him the meaning of the birdsong, the names of trees, the movements of the stars. Picasso fell in love with the freedom of gypsy culture. Years later a poet said, 'In the great nation of the gypsies of art, Picasso is the most gypsy of all.' Picasso took special pleasure from this remark.

Self-Portrait, 1899–1900. By the turn of the century, and not yet out of his teens, Picasso was supremely confident of his ability.

When Picasso returned to Barcelona in 1899, the once-mighty Spanish Empire was finally dead: Cuba was independent and the Philippines had fallen to the Americans. Disabled old soldiers begged in the streets and revolutionary feeling grew. A group of artists – calling themselves the 'Generation of '98' – condemned their '**moribund** society'. Picasso's work took on a darker, morbid hue.

Artists, anarchists, **modernists** and Catalan **nationalists** discussed ideas and held exhibitions and performances in a smoky cabaret bar, Els Quatre Gats (the Four Cats). Many supported the anarchist notion 'destruction is creation!' Picasso was deeply involved and gathered a group of young artists and poets around him. This spirit of revolution created more revolution. At only nineteen Picasso would argue with the leaders of Barcelona's modernists – only in their mid-twenties themselves – and call them outdated!

In 1900, Picasso held his first one-man show at Els Quatre Gats. At about this time he also met the poet Jaime Sabartés. Pablo introduced himself as Pablo Ruiz Picasso. Dazzled by his talent, Sabartés christened him 'Picasso' – a single and unusual name that seemed to suit him best. Sabartés later said 'we spoke of him as of a legendary hero'. Sabartés would do much to perpetuate the Picasso myth.

In 1899, Picasso designed this illustration for the menu at Els Quatre Gats. The bar was a centre for ferocious debate, and almost all of Picasso's closest friends were members of the circle he met there.

The Blue Period

In October 1900, just before his nineteenth birthday, Picasso made his first visit to Paris. He made the journey with a close friend from Els Quatre Gats, a fellow artist called Carlos Casagemas. In preparation for their journey, the friends had identical suits made in black corduroy. Broad, muscular and barrel-chested, Picasso was proud, vain and confident of his physical prowess. He spoke no French and had no place to stay, but other Spanish artists living there helped him find accommodation and a studio. One, a Catalan businessman called Petrus Mañach, was smitten with the dynamic young artist, and agreed to pay Picasso 150 francs a month for his entire output.

Picasso toured art galleries, studying the **Impressionists** and the artist Delacroix – sometimes called 'the first Impressionist' (see page 58). Visiting theatres and music halls, Picasso fell in love with the garish squalor of the entertainers' world and their freedom from responsibility.

Picasso's stay was cut short when he agreed to take Casagemas home to Málaga for Christmas, to help him recover from an unhappy love affair. Picasso's family were displeased with Pablo's wild appearance so he left for Madrid. Casagemas returned to Paris and shot himself dead. The shock of the news gave Casagemas's mother a heart attack and killed her. In Picasso – according to one biographer – it created sorrow, guilt and seething rage. Picasso returned to Paris, taking over his dead friend's studio.

The suicide of Casagemas

For Picasso, art became the means with which he dealt with his experiences. When Casagemas died, he responded to his friend's death through art. Picasso's *Evocation (The Burial of Casagemas)* was full of **symbolism**. Mourners surround a shrouded body while Casagemas rides a white horse towards heaven, embraced by a woman. *Evocation* marked the beginning of Picasso's 'Blue Period'.

The Impressionists

Today, the works of Monet, Renoir, Pissarro, Degas and Manet are among the most recognized in the world. The Impressionists painted quickly, to recreate the effect of light on water, leaves and people, and capture a moment in time in the same way as a photograph. Previous generations of artists had portrayed the 'great and the good', but the Impressionists recorded the lives of ordinary working people. In turn, Impressionism was the first movement of **Modernism**, and led to almost every major artistic movement of the 20th century.

France became the centre of Modernism in literature, drama and sculpture as well as painting.

Woman Ironing, 1904. After the death of Casagemas, Picasso filled his paintings with people on the fringes of society executed in sombre blue tones. In *Woman Ironing*, Picasso captured the physical graft of modern labour. He called her 'a revered martyr of human society'.

> " Many years after Casagemas's death, Picasso took a lover, Françoise Gilot, to a seedy Parisian apartment. He wanted to show her that nothing, not even great beauty, lasts forever. In the apartment a toothless old woman lay dying on a bed. He gestured at her: *'When she was young she was very pretty and made a painter friend of mine suffer so much he committed suicide… She turned a lot of heads. Now look at her.'* "

Depression in Paris

From this time, Picasso was spurred by grief and a sense of exile from Spain. His isolation was emphasized by the fact that he did not speak French at the time and relied on a small group of Spanish-speaking friends. In his work he expressed his solitude in pervasive blue tones. His subjects were victims, trampled by circumstances.

There were other pressures on him, too. He found Parisian winters oppressive, and his relationship with Mañach, who was still buying all his work, worsened. There was no demand for depressing images of suffering and Mañach could not sell Picasso's pictures – but Picasso would not compromise and paint more marketable images. Picasso's depression deepened. In 1902 he turned his back on his growing reputation as an artist in Paris and begged the train-fare back to Barcelona from his father. However, this dependency on others, not least his father, made Picasso's depression worse.

Paris again

In 1904, Picasso returned to and finally settled in Paris. He moved into a dilapidated building in the artists' district of Montmartre. His neighbours – artists, writers, musicians, prostitutes, down-and-outs, crooks – provided Picasso with models for his blue themes. Even so, he never went out alone after dark, or without a gun!

In August, Picasso met a beautiful, intelligent young woman called Fernande Olivier. Later she described him as 'small, black, thickset… with piercing black eyes'. They became lovers, and with Fernande, Picasso found the domestic calm he needed to break his blue mood.

The building where he lived, nicknamed the *Bateau Lavoir* (Laundry Boat), became a magnet for a circle of brilliant friends: the famous painters Henri Matisse, Georges Braque and Marie Laurencin, the poets Max Jacob and Guillaume Apollinaire, and the rich American **bohemians** Leo and Gertrude Stein (see pages 58–9). Picasso put up a sign, 'The Poets' Rendezvous'. Max Jacob later called these 'the most wonderful days of my life'. Picasso would remember them as his golden age.

Picasso in Montmartre, in 1904. A seedy district of Paris, Montmartre soon became famous for its artistic and bohemian residents.

17

The Rose Period

At 24, Picasso was now more confident, and secure in his relationship with Fernande. The sombre blue tones were replaced and a warmer, more vibrant rose hue began to permeate his work. Picasso's choice of colours now included pinks, ivory white, muted greens, blues and yellows.

Picasso visited the nearby *Circus Médrano* up to three times a week. He took the circus folk as his subjects – misfits who seemed to belong everywhere and nowhere. Picasso believed both artists and actors were similar because they both created illusions with which to enchant or provoke their audiences.

Picasso often showed Harlequin standing apart, his expression neutral. In *Family of Acrobats with an Ape* (1905), Harlequin sits beside the young mother, his stillness in stark contrast to the squirming infant on her lap.

His work also revealed an interest in human relationships, especially between people trapped in their theatrical personalities.

Picasso closely identified himself with the character of Harlequin, the unsmiling jester. The melancholic figures of the Rose Period paintings enjoy a shared intimacy and a desire to protect each other from the outside world. Like Harlequin, Picasso saw himself as a tragic-comic misfit, an outsider. He showed Harlequin as a master of trickery and magic, but not of the relationships that make ordinary people happy: a man acting the clown in public whatever his private feelings were.

The Rose Period proved popular with critics and buyers alike. In April 1906, Ambroise Vollard, an important art dealer, bought 30 of Picasso's paintings for 2000 francs – enough to cover household expenses for three years!

Picasso with Fernande Olivier, in 1906. Fernande brought to their relationship the domestic peace and stability Picasso needed to shake off his Blue Period and develop his unique artistic vision.

A visit to Spain

Pablo and Fernande set out for Spain. She later recalled, 'The Picasso I saw in Spain was... less wild, more brilliant and lively... at ease, in fact.' After visiting his family and showing Fernande off to his friends, the pair made their way to the village of Gosol, in the Pyrénées. Close to the borders of Andorra, Spain and France, many villagers made a living from smuggling. Picasso and Fernande spent the days walking in the mountains and the nights listening to the smugglers' tales.

In Gosol, Picasso developed his interest in **classical** themes. In his 'Mediterranean' phase, Picasso painted Fernande again and again, in a style inspired by ancient Greek art. He was also developing an interest in **primitive art**, stimulated by recently unearthed prehistoric Spanish sculptures he had seen in the Trocadéro and Louvre museums. New ideas welled up in a creative frenzy. On his return to Paris, Picasso threw himself into painting, inspired by his Spanish travels. Picasso was about to make his most significant artistic innovation – one that would shake the foundations of European art.

A new language of painting

During Picasso's Rose Period, two works stand out in style and execution – *Portrait of Gertrude Stein* and *Self-Portrait with Palette*. Both demonstrated Picasso's growing interest in the **primitive art** of Africa, Catalonia and the Pacific, and indicated the direction he was about to take.

Self-Portrait with Palette, 1906. This painting and the *Portrait of Gertrude Stein* gave powerful clues as to the direction in which Picasso's art was now heading.

Portrait of Gertrude Stein, 1906. Stein's mask-like face owed much to the ancient religious masks and artefacts Picasso had been studying.

The portrait of Gertrude Stein

Picasso began his portrait of Stein in 1905. He was usually a quick and prolific painter, able to complete a portrait in just one or a few sittings. As the work proceeded, however, Picasso grew increasingly unhappy. In May 1906, after more than 80 sittings, he suddenly painted out the whole head. 'I can't see you any longer when I look,' he exclaimed. His difficulties were part of a growing sense of frustration with the way his paintings could not express what he wanted them to.

After his trip to Spain with Fernande, energized by the 'good air, good water, good milk and good meat' of Gosol, Picasso completed the portrait – without Stein there. The face was mask-like. When people complained she did not look like her portrait, Picasso replied, 'She will!' Gertrude Stein herself was delighted with it. And indeed she did grow to resemble her portrait, as she grew older.

Primitive influences

By 1906, a number of artists were being inspired by artefacts such as masks and primitive statuettes taken from Africa, Latin America and the Pacific Islands. These were highly simplified and very expressive. Matisse wrote of some African statuettes, 'I was struck by their character, their purity of line. It was as fine as Egyptian art. So I bought one... Picasso took to it immediately.'

Shock of the new

Picasso was fascinated by these artefacts and began sketches for *Les Demoiselles d'Avignon*. He completed this painting in 1907, and it marked a great leap forward. The large image he painted of five naked women shows them with jagged and angular limbs and mask-like faces. The picture is groundbreaking because of the way that Picasso distorted his subjects, painting their bodies from impossible perspectives and filling the picture with direct primitive **symbolism**.

Picasso showed *Les Demoiselles d'Avignon* to his friends. 'It's a hoax!' Matisse declared. André Derain (see page 58) thought he was having a mental breakdown: 'Picasso will be found hanging behind his big picture.' Braque was shocked and excited: 'It is as if Picasso has drunk petrol and is spitting fire!'

Picasso believed the painting had its own significance. He thought of it as an act of destruction rather than a piece of art – a casting-out of demons that had possessed him and stifled his own creativity with outdated rules. It was his declaration of war on artistic creation! Then he rolled the canvas up and put it away for nine years. Unseen, its

reputation began to exert an almost mystical power over the art world, as word spread from those who had seen it to those who had not.

Cubism

By 1907, both Picasso and his new painter friend Braque were struggling, in Braque's words, like 'two mountaineers roped together' to find what Picasso described as 'a new language of painting': one that could show four dimensions, including the passage of time, in a two-dimensional art form. 'Imagine,' Braque later explained, 'a man who would spend his life drawing profiles, as if he would have us believe that Man has only one eye.'

It was Braque who first conceived the ideas that would be termed **Cubism**, to which Picasso responded. Though about to launch an artistic revolution, they did not name it themselves. 'Cubism' – like '**Impressionism**' before it – was a derogatory name coined by a critic. Cubism owed much to Paul Cézanne (see page 58), who believed 'everything in nature is modelled on the sphere, the cylinder and the cone'.

This photo of Georges Braque (right) and Fernande Olivier was taken by Picasso. Picasso once compared his and Braque's partnership to the Wright brothers – the pioneers of powered flight. Picasso even re-named Braque 'Wilbur' after one of the Wright brothers.

Inspired by Braque's cubist landscapes of L'Estaque, in the south of France, Picasso spent the summer at Horta del Ebro, in Spain – where he completed a series of his own cubist landscapes. By 1910, Picasso saw himself as a revolutionary. He claimed he was determined to reach the widest audience with his art – even humble peasants and ordinary workers. Despite these claims however, he was very **elitist**. He would be very secretive and enjoyed a childish world where a private language elevated his immediate circle of friends from the masses. Picasso liked to promote himself and his art and many other people were happy to go along with him.

In 1911, Fernande and Pablo spent the summer at Céret, a former monastery in the Pyrénées. Braque joined them. Working together in a studio, Braque and Picasso cajoled and provoked each other to dizzying creative heights. They introduced lettering, snatches of song lyric, shreds of advertising posters and newspaper headlines into their work. Critics were outraged; one confessed he stood in awe of Picasso – but did not understand what he was looking at.

Love changes

When Fernande met and fell in love with a young Italian painter, Picasso first showed his eccentric sense of domestic priorities. He wrote to Braque: 'Fernande left yesterday with a... painter. What will I do about the dog?' Within 24 hours, however, Picasso had replaced Fernande. He lured his new love, Marcelle Humbert, away from her lover – and his good friend – Louis Markus. Marcelle and Pablo fled to Céret, where Picasso renamed her Eva. Later they rented a villa near Avignon. Picasso celebrated their love in works like *Jolie Eva*, *Pablo-Eva* and *Ma Jolie*. He even painted a **still-life** on the villa wall. However, Picasso's reputation was growing and he knew his work was beginning to command good prices from art collectors. He shrewdly had the wall carefully dismantled and sent to his Paris dealer in a packing case.

This was a creative period and Picasso also began to make sculpture. After seeing paper constructions by Braque, Picasso made *Guitar* from sheet metal and wire. A critic asked: 'What is it?' Picasso replied: 'I call it a guitar.' (Picasso retained an interest in guitars as subjects throughout his life and completed many paintings and sculptures based on them.)

Picasso seemed to go from strength to strength. By 1913, he had begun to use vivid colour in a development called '**Synthetic Cubism**'. Over the next few months Braque began to use collage – art that incorporates paper, cloth, string and so on. Picasso responded, using, amongst other things, sand, wood, scraps of old iron and cardboard in his next pieces; things that he said represented the 'waste products of human life'. Collage is a very common artistic technique today, but then it represented an adventurous and very controversial artistic departure.

A changing world

In May, Picasso's father Don José died. Depressed, Picasso spent more time at Céret with Eva. When Eva fell ill, doctors diagnosed bronchitis –

a serious condition at that time. In September, the couple moved to a new Paris home. The view, dominated by the Montparnasse Cemetery, added to Picasso's sense of gloom.

In 1914, Picasso's work was being exhibited in Europe and the USA. At auction a German collector bought Picasso's *Saltimbanques*, which sold for 1000 francs in 1908, for 11,500 francs (equivalent to tens of thousands of dollars or pounds in today's money). This proof of Picasso's popularity provoked fresh outrage in the popular press, much of which hated his art. By 1914, Picasso's reputation had grown beyond the confines of the art world. But that world was about to be blown apart.

Ma Jolie, 1914. Picasso never painted a portrait of Eva Humbert, but there are many references to her as 'Ma Jolie' (my pretty), in his cubist works.

World War I

For years, competition between the empires of France, Britain, Russia, Germany and Austria-Hungary had been growing. In June 1914, Serbian **nationalists** assassinated the heir to the Austrian throne. Austria-Hungary declared war on Serbia. Serbia appealed to Russia for protection. In support of Austria-Hungary, Germany declared war on Russia and its ally France. Germany hoped Britain would remain neutral, but when German troops attacked France through Belgium on 4 August 1914, Britain too declared war.

The most fevered dreams of the European **avant-garde** could not have imagined the blood and mud-drenched horror of World War I. Everything would be changed – forever. By 1918, over 10 million people had lost their lives, over 20 million were injured. The war shattered traditional behaviour and habits: the 19th century was buried alongside the dead.

Many artists, including Apollinaire, Braque and Derain, answered their nation's call to arms. Picasso saw them off at the station. Braque and Apollinaire both suffered serious head injuries and all three men returned irreversibly altered by their experiences. 'I never found them again,' Picasso later wrote.

Death of Eva

As a Spanish citizen, Picasso was not required to do military service. Some thought it wrong that he should avoid it, but friends believed his delicate health excused him. Eva's

Eva Marcelle in 1912. Though she later became seriously ill, she kept the truth from Picasso for fear that he might abandon her.

health, which had never been good, worsened. Afraid Picasso would leave her, she kept its severity secret. When she finally revealed she had **tuberculosis**, Picasso, ever the **hypochondriac**, fled in fear to his old studio in the *Bateau Lavoir*. When Eva died on 14 December 1915, Picasso's art dealer, Daniel-Henry Kahnweiler, blamed him for stealing her away from Louis Markus and exposing her to the intensity of his life.

By Christmas, Picasso was terribly depressed. He moved home and was promptly burgled: it probably hurt more that the thieves ignored his paintings and stole only his linen. The only brightness in his life at this time was meeting the poet Jean Cocteau and Serge Diaghilev, director of the famous Ballets Russes (see page 58).

New collaborations

In 1916, Cocteau asked Picasso to design sets and costumes for *Parade*, a ballet conceived by Cocteau and performed by Diaghilev's Ballets Russes. His designs were a shocking departure from traditional sets and typical of Picasso, who believed rules were made to be broken. Apollinaire was also eager to join in. In the event, the involvement of so many brilliant but fiercely self-centred artists meant the creative process was regularly torn by arguments and fights. *Parade* was almost never made!

Parade

In many ways, *Parade* – based on a fantastically imagined circus – was the riotous dawn of modern art. Erik Satie composed music using typewriters and sirens. While some cheered 'vive Picasso', others booed. Fights broke out. Only Apollinaire, in uniform and with his head bandaged, prevented a riot. Apollinaire later described *Parade* as '**Surrealism**' – the first use of the word. Picasso was labelled 'a dabbler' by the critics: no serious artist, it was believed, would design sets and costumes for a ballet!

Costume design for the ballet *Parade*, 1917. It was a radical departure for an artist of Picasso's stature to be designing for the stage. Picasso himself believed such boundaries were only there to be broken.

Olga Koklova

In February 1917, Picasso met Olga Koklova, a dancer with the Ballets Russes and daughter of an Imperial Russian General. Olga appealed to Picasso's fascination with Russia, and he believed she had an air of Slavic mystery. Olga's attraction to Picasso appears to have been less complex – he had status, fame and wealth.

Picasso also met the controversial Russian composer Igor Stravinsky, as revolutionary an artist as Picasso. In 1913, Stravinsky's ballet *The Rite of Spring* had been so controversial that his opponents and supporters had fought in the aisles and the dancers were booed and hissed!

In July 1918 Picasso and Olga married and moved into a grand new apartment. Though friends had attended the wedding – with Max Jacob and Apollinaire playing ceremonial roles – Olga made it clear that they were no longer welcome at their home.

Seemingly exhausted by his efforts to push back artistic boundaries, Picasso, the most revolutionary artist of the age, sought peace and respect. The **cubist** painter Juan Gris (see page 59), whom Picasso had belittled in the past, wrote to Kahnweiler: 'Picasso still does good things, when he finds time between a Russian ballet and a society portrait.'

Picasso tamed?

Picasso seemed like a tame, shackled bull. He presented the wife of his new dealer, Paul Rosenburg, with a painting of her and her son – and she said she would rather have one by Boldini, a fashionable portraitist. In silence, Picasso painted a second picture in the style she wanted – and signed it 'Boldini'.

On 9 November 1918, just before the end of the war, Apollinaire succumbed to the virulent influenza epidemic sweeping the globe. For Picasso his death was a shock: in many ways it symbolized the end of his old world. The dawning peace represented the birth of the new.

Olga Koklova imposed new conventions on Picasso. When he painted her she said, 'I want to recognize my face!'

29

'Classical Arcadias'

> " *'It's not what an artist does that counts,'* Picasso said, *'but what he is.'* "

By the end of the war, France was in ruins. War debts loomed, and one and a half million Frenchmen were dead. Paris was a shabby, melancholic town. But the city soon revived: as the **Jazz Age** dawned, Paris again became dominant in art and culture. Gertrude Stein said Paris is 'where the twentieth century is'. The celebrity of artists became as important as their art. Picasso and Olga were now caught up in a glittering social whirl.

When Olga banished art from their apartment, Picasso rented another on the next floor and turned it into a studio and store. It was soon full of paintings, African masks, ancient artefacts and books – the accumulation of his past life.

Living the high life

Derain and Braque raged against Picasso's surrender to the high life. Picasso called Braque 'Madame Picasso', claiming his criticisms were like those of a wife, and belittled both Braque's work and his contribution to **Cubism**.

In contrast to *Parade*, Picasso's next ballet commission, *The Three-Cornered Hat*, was a triumph. Picasso radiated self-confidence: he dressed and lived well, and the public acclaimed his work simply because *he* had painted it, silencing those who disagreed. The celebrated figure of Jean Cocteau led Picasso through the society salons and Picasso's name featured on every fashionable guest list. Misia Sert, a brilliant hostess, pulled together the circles of high art and high society. Although his former dealer Kahnweiler had returned to Paris, Picasso decided to stay with Paul Rosenburg, who attracted a 'better' – richer – clientele. However, it was Picasso, rather than any of the dealers, who was increasingly in charge of the sale of his canvases and the prices he would charge.

Picasso also worked on a third ballet, Stravinsky's *Pulcinella*. Despite arguments with Diaghilev, the ballet and Picasso's contribution won critical praise.

Olga Koklova, Picasso and Jean Cocteau in 1917. Picasso surrounded himself with the cream of the artistic **avant-garde**.

Fatherhood

In 1920 Picasso and Olga left Paris for Juan-les-Pins, a fashionable resort on the Mediterranean coast. Olga was now pregnant.

It was here that Picasso developed his neo-classical style. This was based on the human figure, on the art of the high **Renaissance** and on his growing fascination in ancient Roman and Greek art. This interest had first developed when, while designing *Parade* in 1917, he travelled to Italy and visited many of the sites of **classical** antiquity – including Rome, Naples and the buried city of Pompeii. Observing the monumental statues of both Rome and the Renaissance, Picasso was fascinated by their solidity and by the heavy folds of their garments, and tried to capture this effect in his paintings. The neo-classical style was also inspired by Picasso's lasting interest in mythology and the Mediterranean environment around him. The women in his paintings grew massive and solid, their faces impassive masks.

In February 1921, Olga gave birth to a son. Though Picasso was almost 40 years old, Paul (Paulo) was his first child. Picasso recorded his delight in a series of sketches and paintings. However, he increasingly portrayed mother and son as occupying a self-contained world. Revisiting the themes of the Rose Period, Picasso was once more the distant observer, this time of the close bond between mother and child.

In May, Picasso worked on a fourth ballet, *Cuadro Flamenco*, largely to step in for Juan Gris, who had originally been invited to do it but who was unwell and late with his designs. The *Cuadro Flamenco* designs did nothing to enhance Picasso's reputation. Many of his old friends felt alienated, including Gris and Kahnweiler. Max Jacob fumed '[Picasso] is deader than Apollinaire.' However, there were many who were eager to praise Picasso.

Towards Surrealism

While Picasso enjoyed the pleasures of fame and the acclaim of high society, his art did not stand still. A new artistic movement called **Surrealism** had emerged. Picasso was the surrealists' hero, because he was the first artist to be so apparently liberated from rules and conventions. Ironically, they were praising him at a time when he was at his most traditional, continuing to explore classical themes and fascinated by his infant son.

Picasso and Chanel

In 1922, Jean Cocteau asked Picasso to design the sets for his adaptation of *Antigone* by Sophocles. The fashion designer Coco Chanel (see page 58) would do the costumes.

Picasso produced his set two days before the premiere. Using chalk on a huge sheet of crumpled canvas, inspired with classical themes, he created a cave of marble, with three columns. Those watching him work burst into applause. *Antigone* was a triumph – though it was Chanel who stole the headlines.

Both Picasso and Chanel were fascinated by each other. She said of his dark, darting eyes: 'He is like a sparrowhawk.' He admired her rise from poverty in the rural Auvergne region of France to the height of Parisian society.

Surrealism

Surrealism was an art movement that tried to challenge realism in art and literature by using humour, dream and 'counter-logic', or the absurd. Many surrealist pieces attempted to recreate the world of dreams and the subconscious.

Paul Drawing, 1923. After the birth of his first child, Paul, Picasso completed many pictures of him. Not part of any wider artistic vision, they belonged to Picasso's personal life and he kept nearly all of them.

Through 1923 Picasso continued to be celebrated. His name was synonymous with the explosion of wealth, energy, creativity and industry that became known as the 'Jazz Age'. Meanwhile, his family situation lent him an air of domestic bliss. Critics praised the delicate portraits of his infant while Olga's cool, classic beauty lent itself to Picasso's artistic preoccupations. He immortalized her in a much admired series of paintings and drawings.

However, there were cracks beneath the surface.

Picasso and the avant-garde

Picasso was now 42 years old and nearing the height of his fame. But he seemed increasingly disenchanted with his lifestyle and Olga's snobbery and social values. The more obvious his unhappiness with the present, the more violently she tried to erase his past, destroying any letters from friends that mentioned Fernande. As Picasso withdrew into his imagination, her anger grew.

Picasso's own rage found many targets. When he learned that Matisse was designing for the Ballets Russes he raged: 'Matisse! What is a Matisse?' Inspired by the **surrealist** painter André Breton and by the young Spanish surrealist Joan Miró, a spiky quality entered his work. *The Three Dancers*, painted in 1925, was as important a change in painting style as *Les Demoiselles d'Avignon* had been. The painting

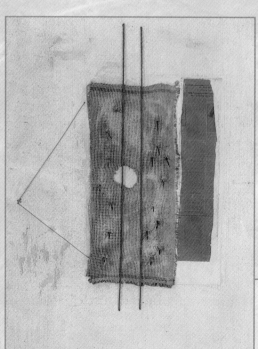

was inspired by the premature death of Picasso's friend Ramon Pichot. He believed that Pichot's health had been destroyed by his love for the same woman who had driven Casagemas to suicide.

At work and play

In 1925 *Les Demoiselles d'Avignon*, originally completed in 1907, was reproduced for the first time in a publication called *The Surrealist*

In 1925, the surrealist artist André Breton proclaimed Picasso as 'one of us'. *Guitar* (1926) was one of several violent and jagged pieces Picasso produced during his surrealist period.

> " *'Give up your easy way of life. Take to the roads.'* "
> André Breton, surrealist artist, 1925

Revolution!. Picasso also joined the first surrealist exhibition that same year. In 1926 he produced another piece called *Guitar*, this time a collage that included nails hammered out through the canvas. (Originally he had wanted to mount razor blades and create a work of art that drew blood when it was touched!) Though celebrated and inspired by the surrealists, however, Picasso kept his distance. He realized his artistic freedom depended on not being labelled as a particular type of artist.

In January 1927, Picasso was wandering the streets of Paris, searching for new artistic inspiration using **automatism** – a surrealist technique to tap into the unconscious mind. Outside the Louvre Museum he met a young woman called Marie-Thérèse Walter. She was seventeen years old. Struck by her beauty and strong athletic posture, Picasso persuaded her to model for him. They soon became lovers. Passion again stirred his imagination: he filled his work with images based on Marie-Thérèse's voluptuous form.

In May, Juan Gris – the third member of the **cubist** partnership, who had inspired the vibrant colours of **Synthetic Cubism** – died. He was

40 years old. With breathtaking **hypocrisy**, considering that he had often criticized Gris's career, Picasso made himself chief mourner at the funeral.

The Red Armchair (1931) featuring Marie-Thérèse Walter. Noticing her outside the Louvre Museum, Picasso exclaimed: 'My name is Picasso – I would like to paint you!'

In July, Picasso, Olga, Paul and a nanny left to spend their annual summer vacation on the Côte d'Azur, on the south coast of France. They were chauffeur-driven everywhere; 'Driving is bad for a painter's wrists,' Picasso claimed, doubtless a sneer at Braque, who loved to drive racing cars. Picasso secretly installed Marie-Thérèse in a house nearby.

Picasso's relationship with Marie-Thérèse broke many taboos – she was very young while he was middle-aged and married with a family – but Picasso considered himself above social conventions. He enjoyed Marie-Thérèse's beauty, but his treatment of her – like many of his models and lovers – revealed a strong streak of **misogyny**.

In 1928 a Spanish friend taught Picasso to weld. Pablo's interest in sculpture grew and he produced a series of wire constructions he described as 'drawings in space'. Picasso's fame was now such that even the **Wall Street Crash** and the onset of the **Great Depression** in 1929 had no impact on prices for his work, and his dealer was still able to sell many pieces.

Ever restless, in 1931 Picasso bought a 17th-century manor house outside Paris. He transformed the stables into a sculpture studio. The world celebrated

Marie-Thérèse Walter with Maya. Maya was Picasso's first daughter and was born when he was 53.

The Minotaur

In 1933, Picasso launched his own surrealist magazine, *Minotaure*. Picasso had become fascinated with the Greek legend of the Minotaur. Half-man, half-bull, the Minotaur represented uncivilized nature, ruled by its own instincts and desires. Picasso saw it as a symbol of his own intense passions and also the entrance of untamed violence in the world. He depicted the violent and amoral life of the Minotaur in a large series of etchings and drawings, often portraying Marie-Thérèse as its victim. The rise of the Minotaur in Picasso's work coincided with the rise of **Nazism** in Germany in 1933. After the start of the **Spanish Civil War** in 1936, it was transformed into a heroic bull.

Picasso's 50th birthday with **retrospectives** of his work in Paris and in Zurich, Switzerland, and numerous articles appraising his work.

A ruined marriage

Picasso could appear to be a charming, modest, family man. But behind this façade he was full of rage and could behave like the violent Minotaur he often depicted in his work. He physically and emotionally attacked Olga, and his affair with Marie-Thérèse became publicly known. By 1935 their marriage was in ruins. When Olga discovered Marie-Thérèse was pregnant, she finally left, taking fourteen-year-old Paul with her. Her refusal to grant Picasso a divorce pushed him into another deep depression.

To help him cope, Picasso persuaded an old friend, the Spanish poet Jaime Sabartés, to abandon his wife and family and join him in France. Picasso later painted Sabartés as a Spanish courtier in a ruff. In many ways Sabartés was a courtier to king Pablo, the butt of his jokes, public cheerleader of his master's genius. Sabartés assumed the role of Picasso's trusted friend and secretary until his death in 1968.

In October 1935, Marie-Thérèse gave birth to Picasso's daughter, Maya. But any new stability in their lives was to be short-lived.

War in Spain

By 1936, Picasso was the most respected artist of the age, and there were major international **retrospectives** in Barcelona and Paris. But the lack of privacy, as well as the end of his marriage, drove him from Paris to his holiday home at Juan-les-Pins with Marie-Thérèse. Despite the collapse of his marriage and the birth of Maya, Picasso treated Marie-Thérèse very much as an occasional lover rather than a close partner. His great interest at this time was in 'found-and-altered' sculpture – taking recognizable objects and combining them with other objects to create completely new forms. To this end, he took to gathering junk – wood, skulls, beach toys – from the beaches and woods around Juan-Les-Pins as raw materials.

Returning to Paris in July 1936, Picasso learned of the outbreak of the **Spanish Civil War**. The Spanish military and **fascists**, led by General Franco, had declared war on their democratically elected **Republican** government. Troops and aircraft from **Nazi** Germany and Fascist Italy supported Franco; the republicans were virtually defenceless. Many sympathetic supporters of the Spanish Republic and democracy – Europeans and Americans – travelled to Spain to fight against Franco.

The influence of Dora Maar

At the same time, Picasso renewed his acquaintance with Dora Maar, a **left-wing** photographer and **surrealist**. She was as different a woman to Marie-Thérèse as Olga had been to Fernande. His interest in her was stimulated by her game of driving a penknife quickly between her gloved fingers into the wood of café tables. Whenever she missed and cut herself, blood stained her gloves. Fascinated, Picasso asked for her gloves as mementoes. Like his other lovers, Maar became a source of artistic inspiration for Picasso. Marie-Thérèse, meanwhile, was increasingly ignored and had to endure seeing her once-favoured image becoming more and more grotesque in Picasso's pictures.

Maar spoke fluent Spanish, so could discuss the situation in Spain with Picasso in his native language. Influential voices had been raised doubting Picasso's commitment to the republic and rumours even circulated that he favoured the military under Franco. Intense, emotional and politically committed, Dora encouraged Picasso to express open vocal support for the legitimate Spanish republican government. In return, they made Picasso honorary director of the national collection of art treasures, at the Prado Museum.

As the civil war continued, Picasso worked on several anti-fascist and anti-Franco themes, including a series of etchings entitled *The Dream and Lie of Franco*. In these works, his Minotaur image was transformed into a heroic bull. In 1937, Picasso was asked to provide a centrepiece for the Spanish pavilion at the World Fair.

As Picasso worked on the huge *Guernica* painting, Dora Maar photographed him at work, charting its progress.

Guernica

Dora helped Picasso find an enormous studio on rue des Grands-Augustins in Paris where he could prepare the work. His initial sketches and ideas were uninspired. Then, on 26 April 1937, news broke of a bombing raid by the German air force of a defenceless town in the Basque region of Spain. The town was Guernica. This atrocity gave Picasso his theme.

Other artists, journalists, photographers and writers visited him as he worked. In a blizzard of action and inspiration, the 8-metre long painting was completed in little over a month. At one point during work on the painting, Marie-Thérèse confronted Dora over his affections, and appealed to Picasso to choose between them. 'I like you both,' he replied. 'You'll have to fight it out yourselves.' While they fought, Picasso painted on.

Of *Guernica*, Picasso said: 'Painting is not done to decorate apartments. It is an instrument of war… against brutality and darkness.' Executed in stark tones of grey, black, charcoal and white, *Guernica* was inspired by the gruesome warscapes of the Spanish artist Francisco de Goya, the epic canvases of the French artist Jaques Louis David (see page 58), and photographs of the devastated town printed in the French daily newspaper *Ce Soir*. The mouth of every man, woman, child, horse and bull screams in pain and terror: the only point of stillness is the corpse of a baby.

As well as *Guernica*, Picasso completed many other canvases that expressed both his feelings of rage and his sense of powerlessness at the deterioration of the situation in Spain.

Guernica, 1937. Here Picasso incorporated many of the themes he had used in previous years, including **Cubism**, Surrealism, Greek mythology and the Minotaur, adding a new, childlike simplicity to his work.

> " 'In Guernica,' Picasso said, 'I have clearly expressed my horror of the military caste that has plunged Spain into an ocean of suffering and death.' "

As war in Europe approached, *Guernica* travelled the world. It was taken to Norway, London and then shipped to the USA where it stayed. Meanwhile, Picasso expressed further anguish with the jagged *Weeping Woman* (1937) and a number of violent **still-lives**. He also found a new **metaphor** for the times – a cat playing with a bleeding bird. Picasso's paintings of Dora became increasingly vicious and tortured.

The fall of Spain

In 1938, Picasso spent summer in Mougins, in the south of France. The eventual downfall of the Spanish Republic was already obvious. Picasso completed several portraits of local people. Many were infused with a barely concealed anger and contempt for humankind's growing inhumanity. One, *Girl with Cockerel*, shows a young woman about to slaughter a rooster she holds across her lap.

In March 1939, the Spanish republican government finally fell and General Franco made himself **dictator**. Picasso could no longer return to the land of his birth. Meanwhile, the world paid him more attention. That year the New York Museum of Modern Art mounted a great Picasso retrospective.

Picasso grew more restless. In 1939, he holidayed on the Mediterranean coast; both Dora and Marie-Thérèse were amazed to discover he had brought them both. From here he travelled to Paris for a funeral but then had his chauffeur drive through the night to see a bullfight in Frèjus.

On 1 September 1939, it was announced that the German army had invaded Poland. Two days later France declared war on Germany. The storm had broken.

World War II

As Hitler prepared to invade Poland, Picasso was in Antibes on the Mediterranean coast, where he painted his last picture in peacetime – *Night Fishing at Antibes*. Then, to escape the political ferment in Paris, Picasso set himself up in a permanent studio in Royan, near Bordeaux, and travelled regularly between there and Paris.

Hostilities in the west started in earnest in April 1940. Determined not to fight a **trench war** for territory measured in metres, Hitler's generals developed 'Blitzkrieg' (lightning-war) – a tactic of rapid, intensive military attack. Helped by the **Allies**' indecision, poor equipment and inadequate leadership, the Germans swept through Western Europe, brushing aside the armies of Belgium, Holland, France and Britain.

Paris in wartime

On 4 June, Paris was bombed and *l'exode* – the escape of the civilian population – began. The British Prime Minister Winston Churchill had

Night Fishing at Antibes, 1939. It shows Dora Maar and André Breton's wife pushing a bicycle, watching fishermen catch fish by the light of lamps.

German troops entering Paris on 14 June 1940. They occupied the city until 1944.

hoped Paris would be defended district by district. Though many in France shared his wish, French military leaders declared Paris an 'open city' and pulled back. Within six weeks the French had signed a humiliating **armistice** with the Germans.

Against the flow of *l'exode*, Picasso now made his way to Paris, with Sabartés in tow. But he found himself increasingly isolated. Close friends had been forced into exile or arrested, or were in hiding. Picasso's own freedom of movement was limited by **Nazi** curfews and travel restrictions. Increasingly Picasso retreated into his studio in the rue des Grands-Augustins that now also became his living accommodation.

Domestically, Dora and Marie-Thérèse had slipped back into their pretence that the other did not exist. In 1942, Picasso completed *L'Aubade*, a sombre piece showing two women uncomfortably aware of each other's presence. That year he also finished a **still-life** that captured the severe deprivation of life under German occupation. *Pitcher, Candle and Casserole* showed an empty jug and pan, and a candle – the symbol of death.

43

Picasso's stance of **resistance** to the Nazis was one of noble aloofness. While not overtly political he kept his distance from the invaders. He also refused invitations of refuge in other countries. Although his presence in Paris was significant to many French citizens as a sign of resistance to the Nazis, he confided to Jean Cocteau: 'Everything will go from bad to worse. It's all broken in us.'

Recognized in cafés where he went to keep warm, Picasso refused German offers of extra fuel: 'A Spaniard is never cold!' Although cut off from much of his money, which was kept in banks in other countries, Picasso was still very wealthy, but he was anxious to share the hardships of ordinary French people.

Work in the war years

Picasso's pictures at this time did not show the war directly, but reflected instead the influence of the German occupation in his use of dark, sombre colours and gloomy, static subjects. He also returned to sculpture, mostly using found metal objects.

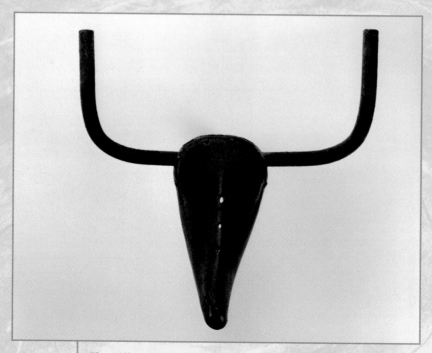

The Bull's Head (1942) is typical of Picasso's 'found-and-altered' pieces: 'One day I found a bicycle saddle in a pile of old junk, and next to it a rusty set of handle bars. Quick as a flash... the idea of this 'bull's head' came to me.'

> " "
> *'I did not paint the war, because I am not one of those artists who go around like photographers to record events. But I have no doubt that the war is contained in the pictures I have painted.'*
> Pablo Picasso, 1945

Picasso was criticized by other painters who were **collaborators**, and forbidden to exhibit his work, but the Germans did not harass Picasso. Although the Nazis labelled him the foremost exponent of 'degenerate art' they still wanted to buy his canvases! The **surrealist** painter Oscar Dominguez even made a living selling forged Picassos to Nazis. On one occasion Picasso distributed postcards of *Guernica* to German officers. One, looking at the picture, asked, 'Is this your work?' 'No' Picasso replied. 'It's yours.'

Françoise Gilot

By 1942, Picasso's relationship with Dora was becoming more discordant. In 1943, dining in a Catalan restaurant, he met Françoise Gilot. Tall, slim and beautiful, she was 20 years younger than Dora and 40 years younger than Picasso, who was now 62. Dora grew increasingly jealous, and although she and Picasso continued to see each other until 1946, separation was inevitable. In one confrontation, she accused Picasso: 'You've never loved anyone in your life. You don't know how to love.' Eventually Dora had a nervous breakdown and left Picasso, rebuilding her life though painting and photography in privacy in Provence.

When Paris was liberated from the Nazis in August 1944, thousands of friends and well-wishers visited Picasso. In October, Picasso's work was the subject of a special exhibition at the Salon d'Automne, in Paris. Up until this point, Picasso had never taken part in the annual French exhibitions of contemporary art.

Picasso's response to war is seen in his art before and after Hitler's war, rather than during it. Following the liberation of Paris, Picasso prepared one of his most important war paintings. He was also about to drop his own political bombshell.

Creating the
Picasso legend

In late 1944, Picasso announced that he had joined the French **Communist** Party. There was a great outcry from some – and celebration from others. Although encouraged by his friend, the **surrealist** poet and communist Paul Eluard (see page 58), he was also attracted by the heroic role Communist Party members had played in the **resistance** movement and the popular respect they commanded after the liberation. 'Were the Communists not the most courageous people in France?' he asked. 'Until the day when Spain can welcome me back, the French Communist Party [has] opened its arms to me and I found in it those that I most value, the greatest scientists, the greatest poets, all those beautiful faces of Parisian insurgents… I am once more among my brothers.'

Eluard also introduced Picasso to Pierre Daix, a communist recently liberated from the **Nazi concentration camp** at Matthausen. Daix told Picasso how the thought of *Guernica* had helped him during his years of imprisonment. Daix later became a close friend and devoted cataloguer of Picasso's work, while Picasso made many contributions to a magazine edited by Daix.

Political paintings

Several of Picasso's paintings of this period have a clear political content, though the number of overtly political works in his total output was minimal. *The Charnel House* was inspired by the revelations emerging about the Nazi concentration camps.

In 1951, Picasso completed *Massacre in Korea* – about the Korean War and based on execution scenes in paintings by Goya and Manet. However, many senior Communist Party officials condemned it for not going far enough in rebuking the Americans for their actions. In 1953 the Soviet **dictator** Joseph Stalin died and Picasso was asked to do a portrait for the French Communist Party newspaper. His picture caused a scandal in the Communist Party for not being realistic enough and Picasso was severely criticized, although Daix stuck by him.

The Charnel House, 1945. This painting features a pile of hideously broken bodies, reflecting scenes from Nazi concentration camps.

Paintings of celebration

Other paintings celebrated not simply the end of the war but also the dawn of a new age and the joy of the living. *Joie de Vivre* (*Joy of Life*) and *Faun Piping* recalled a mythical Ancient Greece populated by nymphs, fauns and centaurs. However, by now the myth of Picasso itself was taking over. According to art historian Timothy Hilton, 'the works of art that he produced for the next 20 years... are interesting primarily because it was Picasso who produced them.'

New directions

Picasso's personal life was as complicated as ever. In 1945, he took his new partner, Françoise Gilot, to his house in Ménerbes. He was also in daily correspondence with Marie-Thérèse until 1946, when he ended his relationship with her and returned to Antibes with Françoise..

In 1947, following the birth of their son Claude, Picasso and Françoise moved into a small house called La Galloise in Vallauris, on the French Riviera. Though he could afford luxury, Picasso seemed not to care about the primitive conditions of the house and the basic sanitation.

Picasso with Françoise Gilot and their son, Claude, at Vallauris. Françoise would later shed an interesting light on Picasso's character as a man.

The little town – largely communist – had once been a centre of pottery making, but the industry was in decline. Single-handedly, Picasso revived the ceramics trade in Vallauris with a period of furious production, creating 2000 pieces of pottery in one year! Many of the pieces were quirky – animal-shaped drinking vessels and jugs, human-faced vases – often in red-brown clay finished in brown and white paint. Local craftsmen produced large quantities of the ceramic pieces he had designed, such was the enormous demand for his work.

> " 'Everything Picasso touched underwent a vital transformation. He brought renewed prosperity to the place he lived and new prestige to the medium in which he worked.' "
> James Lord, art historian, 1993

Mounted Rider, 1951 – a ceramic wine pitcher – was one of the many playful ceramic pieces that Picasso completed in Vallauris.

Lithographs

For several years, Picasso also experimented with lithographic printing techniques, which use ink and water. In 1949, his lithographic image *Dove of Peace* was adopted as the emblem of the International Peace Congress. That same year, his daughter Paloma – Spanish for dove – was born. The revival of bullfighting in southern France after the war and its inevitable associations with Spain rekindled Picasso's enthusiasm for the spectacle. In the 1950s he created a lithographic series of great simplicity and beauty, *La Tauromaquia* (*The Bullfight*).

Picasso took special pleasure in painting his young children at play, reading or lying asleep. Their toys also inspired several sculptures – notably the transformation of one of Claude's toy cars into the head of a baboon.

In 1952, he created his *Temple de la Paix* (*Temple of Peace*) in a ruined chapel in Vallauris. This contained his *War and Peace* murals, a clearly political effort that received much attention from the world's media, raising Picasso's public profile still further.

Françoise leaves

Picasso was constantly in the public eye. Relaxing on the beach he would amuse himself by doodling in the sand, to the fascination of bystanders, and play with his children, pretending not to notice onlookers. But cracks were appearing in his relationship with Françoise. She did not enjoy the unwanted attention of strangers on the beach, nor the uninvited guests who would appear at La Galloise. Three years later she left him – much to Picasso's chagrin. As Cocteau wrote to a friend: 'Picasso likes to do the leaving, not to be left.'

Gilot's memoirs showed Picasso's character in a poor light. She had no doubt he was a genius of electrifying talent, but also a cruel man with a ferocious ego. She described his sadistic need to show off his women as conquests, like a successful bullfighter displaying his kills. Furious, Picasso refused to see her or his children, Claude and Paloma, again or even to acknowledge their existence.

Jacqueline Roque

For Picasso, 1953–54 was a period of self-critical despair with very gloomy and introspective work. In 1954, however, he began a relationship with Jacqueline Roque. His work returned to more outward-looking themes.

Picasso enjoyed his celebrity status, but his fame forced him to leave his homes in Paris and Vallauris. Picasso was so rich he simply locked up his homes and moved to another, leaving everything – furniture, canvases and collections of junk – in place. His new properties grew in size and opulence.

Picasso and Jacqueline moved to a villa they called La Californie, near Cannes, where he worked in the large pigeon loft, often painting the sea view from the window. He also completed 40 variations on Diego Velázquez's *Las Meninas* (*The Maids of Honour*). When his great rival

Jacqueline Roque with Flowers, 1954. The start of Picasso's relationship with Jacqueline Roque inspired in him a new burst of creative energy.

Matisse died in 1954, Picasso completed a series of variations on *The Women of Algiers*, by Delacroix – one of Matisses's idols – in homage. He publicly acclaimed his regard for his rival's originality and greatness: 'All things considered,' Picasso said, 'there's only Matisse.'

In retreat

The bustle and noise of Cannes became oppressive and Picasso and Jacqueline moved to the peace and quiet of Château de Vauvenargues, near Aix-les-Provence. The frequent house moves from the middle of the 1950s were part of Picasso's gradual retreat from public life. Despite age and his increasing isolation, however, Picasso showed no sign of tiring.

Some writers called the paintings he completed in Vauvenargues his 'Spanish' period. During these years, his ties with Spain – a land he had not seen since the 1930s – grew stronger. Spanish visitors told him how popular his work was in his native land. Picasso also published three poems in Spanish.

In 1961 he married Jacqueline (Olga, who had been his legal wife, had died in 1955) and moved to another new home, Villa Notre-Dame-de-Vie at Mougins. Although he celebrated his 80th birthday with feasting, an exhibition, and a bullfight, Picasso lived and worked in relative seclusion at Notre-Dame-de-Vie.

Picasso renewed his interest in monumental sculpture in the early 1960s, cutting and bending huge figures from sheet metal, which was then painted, and sandblasting sculptures from concrete. He also devoted considerable energy to engravings.

The last years

Picasso always drew inspiration from many sources – his artistic contemporaries, the old masters, **primitive** artefacts, myths and legends. Although at the forefront of modern art, he often looked to the past and the works of venerated **Renaissance** artists. In conversations, he frequently ranked himself alongside them rather than his young contemporaries. But many people maintain that the quality of his work from 1945 onward was poor; Timothy Hilton said *Massacre in Korea* was 'so bad as to be

Football Player, 1965. In the 1960s, Picasso renewed his interest in sculpture. Once again these demonstrated his playful sense of humour as well as his acute artistic eye.

embarrassing'. But the quantity of work increased right up to his death. In his eighties he would complete between three and five paintings a day, sometimes working on several simultaneously. Although Picasso's late work was variously described as 'the incoherent scribblings of a frenetic old man,' and the work of 'the most youthful artist alive,' his need to express himself through art was paramount.

Picasso also returned to a favourite theme of the artist's relationship with his model. But now his model, Jacqueline, was also his carer. Picasso hated being physically dependent on her and he sometimes treated her very cruelly as a result. Some of Picasso's final work echoed with the faint images of the African masks that had so startled him in the Trocadéro Museum many years before: 'I must find the mask,' he said.

Picasso and Jacqueline, in 1961. In old age, Picasso became increasingly dependent on Jacqueline's support. She, in turn, became psychologically dependent on him.

To mark Picasso's 85th birthday, the French government organized an international exhibition of 500 works. At 90 years old, he became the first painter to be given a one-man show at the Louvre in the artist's own lifetime.

Pablo Picasso died on 8 April 1973 at his villa in Mougins. He was 91 years old. The estimated value of his estate was over £50 million (US$80 million). Jacqueline Picasso devoted herself to caring for his artistic legacy, as she had his physical welfare, until her death in 1986.

Picasso's legacy

Pablo Picasso was the first truly world-famous artist in the age of mass media. Like the half-man, half-bull Minotaur, he tore through the world of art to put himself, snorting and hoofing the ground, at the forefront of the **modernist** revolution. The irrepressible Picasso helped create widespread artistic awareness and defined the popular image of the artist.

He had a huge and widespread influence on artists. As the British sculptor Henry Moore said: 'Picasso and the British Museum were the only inspiration I needed.' But writers, photographers, journalists, poets and philosophers were also charmed and intrigued by this energetically creative man.

He completed thousands of paintings, etchings, ceramics and sculptures. In his Blue and Rose Periods he created some of the most haunting images ever painted. **Cubism** became the most influential artistic movement of the 20th century. It was a major change in the way artists conceived the idea of painting. Painting was not a representation of the visual world but an expression of the artist's response to it. Cubism inspired artists in many spheres, on many levels: from sculpture to literature, from poetry to fashion and ceramic design. Picasso was a major inspiration for the **surrealists**. Paintings such as *Guernica* (as well as Picasso's political associations) reasserted the political role artists can have in society.

Picasso flirted with the media to promote his art. Whether being photographed working on *Guernica* or filmed in Vallauris, Picasso made himself the subject as much as his art, cultivating the enduring myth of Picasso.

Many artists who followed – Andy Warhol, Roy Lichtenstein, Jackson Pollock, members of 1990s 'Britart' – are famous for their celebrated but controversial styles, with images such as soup cans and dead cows in formaldehyde. But none became as recognizable in so many different styles as Picasso. As the art historian Timothy Hilton said, many artists based their entire careers on what Picasso might have

Picasso at Vallauris, painting a ceramic bowl in 1948. He was always aware of the importance of the role of the media in perpetuating the 'Picasso myth'.

invented and played with for a year or two before moving on to something completely new.

Some accuse Picasso of stealing ideas. In working with contemporaries in Paris, such as Braque, he would naturally have exchanged ideas and found influences. He was also fiercely competitive, sometimes to the point of spitefulness. But Picasso combined his unique perspective and vision with outside influences to create new and totally original art.

As a man, Picasso had deep faults. At times a cruel and tyrannical bully, his treatment of lovers and children was appalling. Few escaped his embrace with their spirits intact: many suffered mental illness, and sometimes even premature death. Was his behaviour a way of hiding deep insecurities about himself?

Throughout his life, Picasso often portrayed his subjects in masks, be they that of the clown, the African mask, or the artist. Indeed, at the end of life he still hunted 'the mask'. But perhaps the mask Picasso looked for but never found was the one he had worn all his life.

Timeline

1881	Pablo Ruiz Picasso born on 25 October in Málaga, in the Spanish province of Andalucia.
1888	Begins to paint under the tuition of his father.
1892	Enters art school at La Coruña.
1895	Moves to Barcelona and enters the School of Fine Arts.
1897	*Science and Charity*. Enrols at Royal Academy, Madrid.
1899	Makes contact with the artistic **avant-garde** in Barcelona.
1900	Visits Paris; shares a studio with friend and fellow artist Casagemas. Agrees to sell his paintings to Petrus Mañach.
1901	Paints *Yo Picasso* and *Child Holding a Dove*. Casagemas commits suicide in Paris; beginning of the Blue Period. Paints *Evocation (The Burial of Casagemas)*.
1904	Settles in Paris. Moves to the *Bateau Lavoir*. Meets Fernande Olivier who becomes his lover until 1911. Paints *Woman with a Crow, Woman Ironing*.
1905	Beginning of the Rose Period – Paints *Family of Acrobats with an Ape, Boy with a Pipe, At the Lapin Agile*.
1906	*Self-Portrait with Palette, Portrait of Gertrude Stein*.
1907	Paints *Les Demoiselles d'Avignon* but immediately hides it away and it is not seen in public for many years. Meets Georges Braque. Dawn of **Cubism**: paintings include *The Dryad* (1908), *The Reservoir at Horta De Ebro* (1909), *Violin and Grapes* (1912), *Ma Jolie* (1914).
1912–13	Makes *Guitar*. This inaugurates a new form of sculpture.
1913	Death of Picasso's father; beginning of **Synthetic Cubism**.
1917	Designs costumes and sets for *Parade*. Meets Olga Koklova. Sketches include a portrait of Stravinsky.
1918	Olga and Picasso marry.
1920	Paints *Still-Life on a Table*
1921	Birth of son Paul (Paulo). *Three Musicians, Seated Nude Drying her Foot, Mother and Child*. Other works include *Women Running on the Beach (The Race)* (1922), *Paul Drawing* (1923), *Portrait of Olga* (1923), *Paul in a Clown Suit* (1924).

1925	Picasso takes part in first **surrealist** exhibition. *Les Demoiselles d'Avignon* reproduced for the first time. Paints *The Three Dancers*.
1927	Meets Marie-Thérèse Walter.
1928–31	Sculptures *Wire Constructions* (1928–9). Picasso's surrealist painting phase includes: *Seated Bather* (1930), *Figures by the Sea (The Kiss)* (1931).
1935	Birth of daughter Maya.
1936	Outbreak of the **Spanish Civil War**. **Retrospectives** of Picasso's career in Barcelona, Madrid, Paris and London. Begins relationship with Dora Maar.
1937	Paints *Guernica, Weeping Woman, Portrait of Dora Maar*.
1939	Paints *Cat Devouring a Bird* and *Night Fishing at Antibes*. World War II begins.
1940–44	Spends the war years in occupied Paris.
1942	Sculpture *Bull's Head*.
1944	Joins the **Communist** Party of France. Sculpture *Man with a Sheep*.
1945	Begins relationship with Françoise Gilot. Paints *The Charnel House*.
1947	Settles in Vallauris and makes many ceramic pieces. Birth of son Claude.
1949	Daughter Paloma born.
1951	Sculpture *Baboon and Young*.
1954	Begins relationship with Jacqueline Roque. Paints *Jacqueline Roque with Flowers*.
1955	Picasso retrospective tours Paris, Munich, Cologne and Hamburg. Paints *Women of Algiers* (after Delacroix).
1957	Paints *Las Meninas*. Completes *La Tauromaquia*.
1961	Marries Jacqueline Roque. Becomes more reclusive in lifestyle. Paints *Déjeuner sur l'herbe* (after Manet).
1968	Jaime Sabartés dies. Completes prints of *The Artist and his Model*.
1973	Picasso dies on 8 April, in Mougins, from complications caused by influenza.

Key creators

The following people feature in the story of Picasso's life, either as contemporaries or as inspiration for his art.

Apollinaire, Guillaume (1880–1918) French poet, writer and art critic; leader of Parisian movement rejecting traditional rules of poetry. His approach was compared to Cubism.

Braque, Georges (1882–1963) French painter credited along with Picasso with developing Cubism.

Breton, André (1896–1966) Radical poet and writer, and founder member of the surrealist movement. In 1930 he joined the Communist Party.

Cézanne, Paul (1839–1906) Post-Impressionist painter and forerunner of Cubism.

Chanel, Gabrielle 'Coco' (1883–1971) French *haute-couture* fashion designer, perfumer and jeweller.

Cocteau, Jean (1889–1963) Incredibly prolific poet, playwright, artist and film-maker. Sponsor of Picasso, Stravinsky, Diaghilev and the Ballets Russes.

David, Jacques Louis (1748–1825) French painter famous for his massive paintings on classical themes. Enthusiast for the French Revolution and later appointed court painter by Napoleon.

Delacroix, Eugène (1798–1863) French painter and leader of the Romantic Movement. Sometimes called the 'first Impressionist'.

Derain, André (1880–1954) Painter, theatre designer and book illustrator. Most famous for his 'Fauvist' paintings, when he was closely associated with Matisse.

Diaghilev, Serge (1872–1929) Ballet manager who worked with some of Europe's greatest names in music, art and dance.

Eluard, Paul (1895–1952) Poet and founder of the surrealist movement in literature.

Gauguin, Paul (1848–1903) Post-Impressionist painter. His work was inspired by his hatred of civilization and his intense feelings for the ways of primitive peoples.

Goya, Francisco de (1746–1828) Spanish painter in the court of Charles IV. His etchings include *The Disasters of War* depicting the atrocities committed during the Napoleonic invasion of Spain.

Greco, El (1541–1614) ('The Greek') Nickname of Domenikos Theotokopoulos. Settled in Spain and became a portrait painter. His best-known work is *Burial of Count Orgaz*. Picasso paid homage to it in his *Evocation (The Burial of Casagemas)*.

Gris, Juan (1887–1927) Pseudonym of José Victoriano González, a Spanish-born painter and exponent of Synthetic Cubism.

Ingres, Jean Auguste Dominique (1780–1867) French painter and leading light of neo-classical painting who tried to reproduce the structure, proportions and form of ancient Greek and Roman art.

Jacob, Max (1876–1944) Poet and writer, and one of the first French artists to befriend and champion the talent of young Picasso.

Laurencin, Marie (1885–1956) French painter and print-maker. Influenced by both the *Fauves* (such as Matisse, Cézanne and Gauguin) and cubists.

Manet, Edouard (1832–1883) Impressionist painter who scandalized the French art world with his painting *Déjeuner sur l'herbe*.

Matisse, Henri (1869–1954) Famous for his vivid use of primary colours, he was also influenced by Cubism and Impressionism.

Miró, Joan (1893–1983) Spanish surrealist and abstract artist.

Monet, Claude (1840–1926) Leading light of Impressionism.

Pissarro, Camille (1830–1903) Leading member of the Impressionists.

Raphael (1483–1520) Italian painter strongly influenced by Michelangelo and Leonardo Da Vinci. His greatest works are in the Vatican.

Stein, Gertrude (1874–1946) American-born writer who settled in Paris and involved herself in the world of experimental art and writing. Her writing was influenced by Cubism.

Toulouse-Lautrec, Henri (1864–1901) French painter and lithographer. In Paris he immortalized in paint prostitutes, dancers, cabaret acts, actors and circus performers and barmaids.

Van Dyck, Anthony (1599–1641) Belgian painter and portrait artist.

Van Gogh, Vincent (1853–1890) Post-Impressionist painter who had a profound influence on subsequent generations of painters.

Velázquez, Diego (1599–1660) Spanish painter in the court of Philip IV, painted many notable portraits.

Glossary

Allies refers to those countries in alliance against Germany in World War II. These included the UK, France, Australia, the USA and the Soviet Union.

anarchism political theory that claims that any organized government system is oppressive

armistice peace treaty signalling the end of a conflict

automatism surrealist technique of painting or writing by 'emptying the mind' and letting the pen be guided by the subconscious

avant-garde pioneers or innovators in any sphere of the arts

bohemian socially unconventional, free-and-easy person; term especially used to describe artists and writers

bordellos brothels employing several prostitutes

classical art of Ancient Greece or Rome, or art in that style

collaborators people, in all walks of life, who actively aided or otherwise helped the German occupying forces in World War II

communist believer in a political philosophy that has at its heart the idea of equality for all, and communal ownership of all property; associated with the writings of Karl Marx and the 1917 revolution in Russia

concentration camp camp used extensively by the Nazis where political opponents, dissidents, racial minorities and others were sent to do hard labour or be put to death

Cubism attempt to show all four dimensions – height, width, depth and time – in a two-dimensional art form. Cubism allowed the examination of an object from a variety of viewpoints, rather than the single viewpoint of traditional painting. This implied change or movement and so also introduced the idea of the passing of time.

curator keeper of a museum or art collection

dictator leader of a country who rules with unrestricted authority. Franco and Hitler were dictators.

diphtheria once common and often fatal infection of the throat and larynx

dyslexia disorder in which a person finds it hard to decipher numbers and letters correctly

elitist person who believes in the dominance of or reliance on a select group of people

fascist supporter of Fascism, a form of extreme dictatorship, characterized by aggressive nationalism and anti-communism

Great Depression worldwide economic collapse which followed the Wall Street Crash and contributed to, amongst other things, the rise of Nazism in Europe and World War II

Great Masters collective name given to the great painters of the Renaissance, the Spanish and French royal courts and the great painters of Holland and Belgium

hypochondria when a person is obsessed with their health, often thinking they are ill when they are not

hypocrisy pretence or simulation of virtue or goodness

Impressionism artistic movement in France which, from the 1860s, rejected the dark tones of studio painting and tried to capture the brilliant effects of sunlight, shadow, water and fog

Jazz Age period of wealth, freedom and hedonism between the end of World War I and the beginning of the Great Depression

left-wing describes someone with extreme socialist political views

metaphor device in language or art where something is represented in terms of something else

misogyny hatred of or contempt for women

Modernism term used to describe the bold experiments in every sphere of artistic activity during the early part of the 20th century

monarchy political system based on kingship and hereditary rule

moribund when something lacks vitality or is at the point of death

nationalist person who believes in the liberation of their country from invader or foreign rulers. It can also refer to someone who puts the interest of their nation and national group above all else, and turns against outsiders, foreigners and minorities.

Nazism term which comes from the National Socialist German Workers' Party, a political party founded in 1919, led by Adolf Hitler. Nazis believed in nationalism, racism and the power of the state over the individual.

primitive art art and sculpture of the pre-conquest peoples of Latin America, Africa and the Pacific, and the prehistoric peoples of Europe. Often simplified, this art usually had religious rather than artistic purposes.

Renaissance term used to describe the period of great discoveries in learning and art which took place in Europe, and especially Italy, in the 14th, 15th and 16th centuries

republican follower of a system of government that relies on elected heads of state

resistance collective name given to all the forms of opposition to the German occupation in World War II: military action, industrial sabotage, propaganda, 'resistance of the mind', unco-operativeness

retrospective exhibition looking back at the work of a particular artist to show how their work developed over their lifetime

socialism political theory that believes in a more equal distribution of income and resources, and in state intervention to control and direct economic activity

Spanish Civil War conflict that engulfed Spain when the Spanish army, aided by Fascist Italy and Nazi Germany, rebelled against the elected Republican government in 1936

still-life painting of an arrangement of one or several inanimate objects, such as fruit, flowers, vases and crockery, musical instruments

Surrealism artistic movement outlined in 1924 by André Breton. It was based on the absurd, heightened and distorted reality, on dreams and the work of the psychiatrist Sigmund Freud.

symbolism use of symbols, sculptures or objects as a way of concentrating or intensifying meaning

Synthetic Cubism development of Cubism, involving larger more understandable abstract forms and colours, creating shapes that were recognizable as familiar objects, such as a mandolin or a guitar. It also encompassed the use of collage.

trench war war fought between armies from fixed positions and fortifications

tuberculosis also known as TB, a serious, once often fatal, lung infection

Wall Street Crash collapse of prices on the New York Stock Exchange in October 1929, which heralded the start of the Great Depression, a worldwide economic collapse

Places of interest and further reading

Places to visit

Because Picasso was so prolific, many museums and art galleries around the world hold examples of his work. These include:

The Art Gallery and Museum, Glasgow, Scotland

Art Gallery of New South Wales, Sydney, Australia

Birmingham City Museum and Art Gallery, Birmingham, UK

Musée Picasso, Paris, France – holds 203 paintings, 191 sculptures, 85 ceramics and 3000 drawings and engravings. For a virtual tour visit www.tamu.edu/mocl/picasso/news/musee

Museo del Prado, Madrid, Spain – *Guernica* can be seen here.

Museum of Modern Art (MoMA), New York, USA, www.moma.org – has many works by Picasso, including *Les Demoiselles d'Avignon*.

The National Gallery of Art, Washington DC, USA, www.nga.gov/collection/collect.htm – has many fine works by Picasso.

On-line Picasso Project, www.tamu.edu/mocl/picasso – lists Picasso museums around the world as well as giving a comprehensive guide to his life and work.

The Tate Modern, London, UK, www.tate.org.uk

Sources

Pablo Picasso: Life and Work, Elke Linda Buchholz, Beate Zimmermann (Könemann, Cologne 1999)

Picasso, Timothy Hilton (Thames and Hudson, London 1996)

Picasso: Creator and Destroyer, Arianna Stassinopoulos Huffington (Weidenfield and Nicholson, London 1988)

Picasso, Hans L.C. Jaffé (Abrams Publishers, New York 1983)

Picasso and Dora – A Memoir, James Lord (Phoenix Giant, London 1997)

Picasso – Portrait of Picasso as a Young Man, Norman Mailer (Hamlyn, London 1975)

Picasso, Roland Penrose (Phaidon Press, London 1991)

The Essential Pablo Picasso, Ingrid Schaffner (Wonderland Press, New York 1998)

Picasso and his Art, Denis Thomas (Hamlyn, London 1975)

Index

Titles in the *Creative Lives* series:

Hardback   0 431 13985 7

Hardback   0 431 13982 2

Hardback   0 431 13983 0

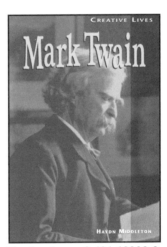

Hardback   0 431 13980 6

Hardback   0 431 13981 4

Find out about other Heinemann resources on our website www.heinemann.co.uk/library